Helen Keller

Nigel Hunter

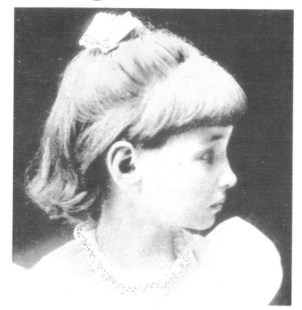

Illustrations by Richard Hook

The Bookwright Press
New York · 1986

Great Lives

William Shakespeare
Queen Elizabeth II
Anne Frank
Martin Luther King, Jr.
Helen Keller
Ferdinand Magellan
Mother Teresa
John F. Kennedy

First published in the United States in 1986 by
The Bookwright Press
387 Park Avenue South
New York, NY 10016

First published in 1985 by
Wayland (Publishers) Limited
61 Western Road, Hove
East Sussex BN3 1JD, England

2nd impression 1986
3rd impression 1987

ISBN 0–531–18031 X
Library of Congress Catalog Card Number: 85–71721

Phototypeset by Kalligraphics Ltd
Printed by G. Canale & C.S.p.A., Turin, Italy

Contents

A life of achievement

USA
15c

HELEN KELLER
ANNE SULLIVAN

The stamp issued on June 27, 1980 to mark the 100th anniversary of Helen Keller's birth. It shows Helen and her teacher Annie Sullivan.

Helen Keller, deaf and blind from early childhood, grew up to be admired throughout the world. She was famous for her achievement in overcoming her handicaps, and for leading a life dedicated to helping others. Everybody who met her was enchanted by her joy in life and felt inspired by her example. From her childhood at the end of the last century to her death as a very old lady, Helen Keller was celebrated as a wonder.

She numbered many well-known people among her friends, and kings, queens and presidents received her as an honored guest. But Helen's deepest sympathies always lay with ordinary people, the world's disadvantaged, the handicapped, the poor and the oppressed.

Without the assistance of her teacher, Anne Sullivan Macy, Helen's achievements might never have become possible. For fifty years the two women lived side by side. With sisterly devotion, Annie guided Helen's life and helped her to communicate with other people.

Helen with her devoted teacher and lifelong friend, Annie.

One of Helen's friends was Mark Twain, the author of *Tom Sawyer* and *Huckleberry Finn*. He said Helen and her teacher formed a "perfect whole" together – that they were almost like one personality. Without Annie, Helen might never have written books, or appeared in films, theaters and lecture halls throughout America. She might never have toured foreign countries and been cheered by large crowds. She might never have been able to do anything to improve the lives of other blind and deaf people. She might never have become known at all . . .

"From light to darkness"

Helen was born on June 27, 1880, in Alabama. Her mother, Kate Adams Keller, had been a "Southern belle" and came from a family with high social standing. She was an early supporter of women's rights. Helen's father, Captain Keller, had been a soldier in the Civil War (1861–65), and was now U.S. Marshal for the northern district of Alabama. The family lived in a small country town called Tuscumbia. Their home was spacious and comfortable, and stood beside fields at the end of a dirt road.

On her first birthday, Helen is said to have clambered off her mother's lap to walk eagerly up to a sunbeam, and a few months later, she was beginning to talk. Then, in February 1882, she was struck by an unidentified illness, with violent pain and high fever which shattered her senses. She lost the use of her eyes and ears. Helen's world became a dark, silent place.

The house in Tuscumbia where Helen was born.

Tears of anger and despair

Helen became a difficult child to live with. Later, she admitted she had been a "wild, destructive little animal." The little girl was often filled with anger, hitting out and kicking at things in tearful rage.

Once, she pinched and chased her Grandma, and her uncle banned her from the house! He said Helen should be sent away to a hospital for the mentally handicapped.

Some of Helen's relatives agreed with her uncle. But others disagreed, and one aunt in particular found Helen loving and lovable. She saw that the little girl had great intelligence. But was there any way to reach her mind, she wondered.

Then Captain Keller decided to ask for help from the Perkins Institution for the Blind, in Boston. The director of Perkins, Michael Anagnos, wrote to Anne Sullivan, who had formerly been a pupil at the institution. He told her about Helen and asked her if she would like to travel a thousand miles south, to Tuscumbia in Alabama, to become Helen's teacher.

Helen's inability to communicate sometimes made her hit out in anger and despair.

Hope for Helen

Anne Sullivan had recently finished her schooling at the Perkins Institution, leaving with high honors. She was twenty years old, and looking for a job. She was excited by the idea of teaching a deaf-and-blind child, and quickly agreed to Captain Keller's terms. She would come to Tuscumbia to live as a member of the family.

Annie had lost her own family when she was a child. She had

Annie at the age of fifteen.

Helen was seven when Annie arrived.

known many years of poverty and suffering. Her mother, sister and brothers had died and her father and another sister had become strangers. For six years, until she was fourteen, she had lived amidst death and deformity at Tewksbury Almshouse, a home for the poor, the crippled, the sick and the mad. When the men lined up for dinner at the almshouse, the women would crowd to the windows to watch them, crying out, "The Horribles, The Horribles!"

Annie longed to leave this terrible place and to receive an

Annie and Laura Bridgman "talking" together, using finger movements.

education. Because of her poor eyesight, she was admitted to the Perkins Institution. There, she developed a fine intelligence and a strong character. She became a great favorite of Michael Anagnos, and a friend of Perkins' most famous resident, Laura Bridgman.

Laura was a deaf-and-blind woman who, fifty years before, had been taught to understand language by touch. People had not believed this could be done, and Laura Bridgman was celebrated as a marvel. The two women "talked" together, using the "manual alphabet," which involved quick finger-movements across each other's hands. The author Charles Dickens had met Laura Bridgman in 1842, and had written about her in *American Notes*. When Kate Keller read this book it gave her hope for Helen – perhaps her daughter might become a second Laura Bridgman?

"Teacher" arrives

Annie arrived in Tuscumbia on March 3, 1887. She found Helen standing in a warm patch of sunlight outside her family home, where the sweet scent of honeysuckle filled the air. Eagerly, she embraced the little girl. Helen struggled to get free: she wanted to search through the newcomer's luggage for something good to eat, and she began kicking out in fury when her mother took the bag away from her. Annie managed to calm Helen's temper by interesting her in the spring-back workings of a watch and the two of them went together into the house.

Upstairs, Annie unpacked a present for Helen. Then, using the special alphabet, she spelled into the child's hand the word D-O-L-L. Before long, Helen was copying the hand-sign. Although she could not make the connection between the movements of her fingers and the doll in front of her, to Annie this was an encouraging start. Soon, Helen knew the signs

for C-A-K-E, as well.

But before she could teach language to Helen, Annie faced another challenge. She felt she had to overcome Helen's wilfulness, and gain her love. There followed great battles of will between the two, especially over Helen's table manners. Helen had always been allowed to eat with her hands, and to take from anybody's plate anything she wanted. But Annie believed she should behave as much as possible like everybody else. Her firmness over this (and over getting Helen to brush her hair, button her shoes, or wash her hands) often brought on Helen's wild temper, and her tears.

It was agreed that the little girl and her teacher should move to a small garden house a short distance away, where Annie would have complete control over her charge. They were alone together day and night, and within a week Annie reported success. She had, with a mixture of firmness and affection, forged a bond between them. Helen had become an obedient, gentle child.

W-A-T-E-R

Helen and Annie moved back into the family house. Helen learned how to sew, and enjoyed doing gymnastics with her teacher. She was never afraid to run around with other children, and Annie encouraged her adventurous spirit. All the time, she spelled into Helen's hand words to describe the world that the little girl could not see or hear. And every day, Helen learned how to spell new words – but she still had no understanding of what they meant.

Then one day, just a month after Annie's arrival, Helen made the vital connection. They had been working on the words "mug" and "water," and Helen had been confusing one with the other. Walking by the well-house, Annie took her across to the gushing pump, and thrust her hand under it, spelling again: W-A-T-E-R.

Suddenly, it flashed into Helen's mind that this meant the wonderful cool "something" that was flowing over her hand. She would always remember the moment, and later wrote: "I left the well-house eager to learn.

Helen would spell out the words with her fingers when she was reading to herself.

Everything had a name, and each name gave birth to a new thought. As we returned to the house every object which I touched seemed to quiver with life."

She knew now what words were. Annie had given her a key to language. At last she had a means of expressing her thoughts and talking to people. For seven-year-old Helen, the world had begun to blossom.

"Sunshine and roses"

Once she came to understand words, Helen's progress was astonishing. Some people called it a miracle. She was extremely quick to learn new words. She learned what it was to think, and what people meant by the mysterious word "love": "The beautiful truth burst upon my mind – I felt that there were invisible lines stretched between my spirit and the spirit of others," she wrote later.

Using words printed in raised letters, Annie next taught Helen how to read and write. They spent the summer outdoors, where Helen delighted in the countryside and in all the insects and animals, flowers and fruit trees. Annie's teaching, and her descriptions of the woods and fields around their home, gave Helen unbounded pleasure.

Then Annie told her about other blind girls at the Perkins Institution, and in September Helen wrote them a letter: "Helen and teacher will come to see little blind girls. Helen and teacher will go in steam car to Boston."

"No ordinary child"

By the time Helen set out for Boston, the following summer, many people had begun to take an interest in her education. With her mother and her teacher, she stayed a few days in Washington, and met President Cleveland at the White House. Also, for the second time, she met Alexander Graham Bell (the inventor of the telephone). Bell was particularly interested in the teaching of the deaf and it was he who had prompted Captain Keller to contact the Perkins Institution, two years before. What a change he saw in Helen now!

At Perkins, where she was often to stay over the next few years, Helen quickly made friends with the other blind children. She was overjoyed when she found that they too knew the manual alphabet, and she loved to talk and play with them.

Michael Anagnos was already a friend. Helen had written him letters, and in the previous spring he had visited the family in Tuscumbia. He was proud of Annie's success in teaching Helen, and he was charmed by the little girl herself. Already, he believed that Helen's achievements would be even greater than Laura Bridgman's.

The inventor Alexander Graham Bell was particularly interested in finding new and better methods of teaching deaf people because his own wife was deaf. He is seen here opening the first telephone line between Chicago and New York.

Blossoming out

Helen visited many places of historical interest in New England. She was also thrilled to go in the ocean, despite the shock of being swept off her feet at

Helen (bottom left) made friends with other deaf-and-blind children at Perkins. She worked to raise money to help little Tommy Stringer (bottom right).

first. "Who put salt in the water?" she asked in surprise. She began to learn French and Latin and her sweet, loving character and joy in life won her friends wherever she went.

They returned home at the end of the year. During the summers that followed, Helen and her family sometimes stayed at a cottage situated among wooded mountains not far from Tuscumbia. By day, there were the woods to explore, and sometimes in the evenings visiting hunters would sit around the campfire telling stories. Other favorite pastimes for Helen included riding her pony, Black Beauty, and playing with her dog, Lioness.

She was developing a great interest in zoology, and also a passion for poetry. Through letters and visits, she came to know two famous writers of the time, John Greenleaf Whittier and Oliver Wendell Holmes. She learned how to read books printed in Braille (a form of type in raised dots, which blind people can read by touch), and was forever reading something new. And soon, she began writing poems and stories herself.

"The Frost King"

At the end of 1891, when Helen was eleven, she sent Mr. Anagnos a fairy story she had written, called *The Frost King*. It concerned King Frost and the colors of autumn: "he paints the leaves with gold and crimson and emerald, and when his task is done the trees are beautiful enough to comfort us for the flight of summer." The story told how this first came about, with mischievous fairies, King Sun and melted treasure all playing a part.

This seemed Helen's most startling achievement yet, and Anagnos printed the story for others to read. But then people noticed how similar it was to a story called *The Frost Fairies*, by Margaret Canby. It now began to look as if Helen and Annie were cheating, in calling *The Frost King* Helen's own composition.

Helen was closely questioned by Anagnos and eight other people, who tried to discover whether she knew *The Frost Fairies* and had merely rewritten the story as *The Frost King*.

A bitter experience

Helen protested her innocence. "I love the beautiful truth," she said. She claimed that it was Annie's descriptions of the autumn countryside that had fired her imagination, and that she had not known Margaret Canby's story. But it was found that a friend of Annie's could have read *The Frost Fairies* to Helen a few years earlier.

It seemed possible that Helen had forgotten all about the story, but it had stayed at the back of her mind ever since.

In any case, this was a most distressing experience for Helen. She felt she could never know for sure whether anything else she wrote was her own composition, or whether it was somebody else's, which she had read and then forgotten.

Also, the confusion and uncertainty meant the end of her friendship with Anagnos, for he later came to believe that Annie and Helen had meant to deceive him. *The Frost King* would remain an unhappy and bitter memory for Helen for many years.

New directions

With the help of a specialist teacher, Helen was beginning to learn how to speak. Many people found her speech hard to follow – though Annie always knew what she was saying – but over the years Helen's voice continued to improve.

She had also started to work for the welfare of others. She began a fund for the education, at Perkins, of a little boy named Tommy Stringer, who, like her, was deaf and blind. And she also helped in Dr. Bell's campaign for the teaching of speech to the deaf.

After the publication of *My Story*, which she wrote for a magazine in 1893, Helen became even more widely known. She and Annie lived mainly in Boston now. They traveled to Washington for the President's inauguration, to the Chicago World's Fair, and to Niagara Falls. Helen enjoyed sailing and canoeing, and visiting the theater, museums, and art galleries – especially when she could touch the sculpture. Everywhere, she delighted in making new discoveries.

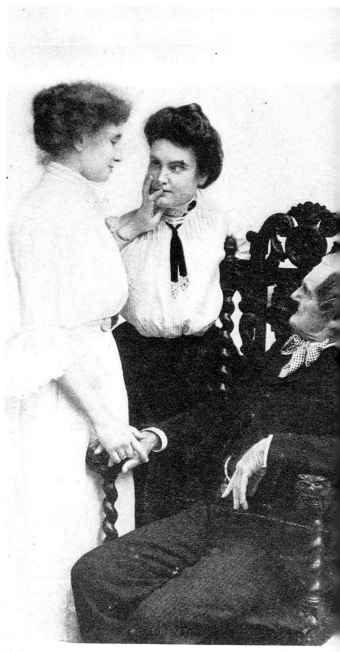

Helen "talking" with Annie and a friend (the actor Joseph Jefferson). She was able to "hear" conversation through her fingers by placing them on the speaker's lips and throat.

A hardworking student

Writing on her typewriter.

history and English literature. Annie, who remained beside her all the time, "spelled" the lessons into her hand, and spent long hours reading to her from books not printed in Braille. Of the books which Helen could read for herself, she was most deeply moved by the Bible and the works of Shakespeare.

The goal which Helen had set herself was achieved in 1899, when she passed the entrance exam to Radcliffe College.

For two years, Helen lived in New York City, attending a school for the deaf. Apart from her work in voice-training and lip-reading (feeling the speaker's lips with her hand), she found that learning German gave her the greatest pleasure. In New York, too, she first met Mark Twain, who was to become a close friend.

At sixteen, Helen entered the Cambridge School for Young Ladies, in Massachusetts. Working alongside the other students, who were neither deaf nor blind, she took courses in German, Latin, arithmetic,

"The Story of My Life"

At Radcliffe, Helen studied alongside some of the most brilliant young women of the day. "Of her fame we are proud / And we shout it aloud," her classmates recited – "While her English we mention with awe!"

To enable Helen to succeed as well as she did, Annie had to work hard. To Helen, it was a great regret that there was so little time to take part in the social activities enjoyed by other students.

In 1901, Helen agreed to write about herself for the *Ladies' Home Journal*. She and Annie were introduced to John Macy, a young writer and editor who helped them with the work. He arranged for Helen's writings to be published in a book, which came out in 1903. The book was called *The Story of My Life*. It has since become a classic. Using letters, reports, and her work for the *Journal*, the book showed Helen's education from childhood. "Knowledge is happiness," she wrote.

Political progress

Reading in her room, which she decorated with a huge red flag.

In an essay called *Optimism*, which she wrote in 1903, Helen looked forward to a time when there would be "no England, no France, no Germany, no America, no this people or that, but one family, the human race; one law, peace; one need, harmony; one means, labor; one taskmaster, God."

Conflicts involving the United States in Cuba, in the Philippines and in Panama had deepened her interest in political issues. In her work for the blind and the deaf, she strongly recommended a program of industrial training. "A human being who does not work is not a member of society and can have no standing in it," she said.

Helen graduated from Radcliffe in 1904, with honors. John Macy, who had helped with Helen's book, continued to spend much of his time with the two women, and in 1905 he and Annie were married.

In another book, *The World I Live In*, Helen explained how she used her imagination to "complete" the world she knew only through smell, taste and touch.

In 1909, Helen joined the Socialist Party. To some people, Helen's political views seemed too radical, but she was determined to speak out on all the important issues of the day. She supported women's suffrage (the right to vote), and birth control, and she spoke out against the use of child-labor and capital punishment. She supported the militant trade unionists, the "Wobblies," in their struggle for workers' rights, and she linked unemployment among the blind and deaf with unemployment among workers as a whole.

In her room she hung up an enormous red flag to show her support for socialism. A collection

She graduated from Radcliffe with honors.

of her socialist writings, called *Out of the Dark*, was published in 1913. She was greatly angered by the reaction of some critics, who said that she could not really know enough to have such firm political opinions.

23

Public appearances

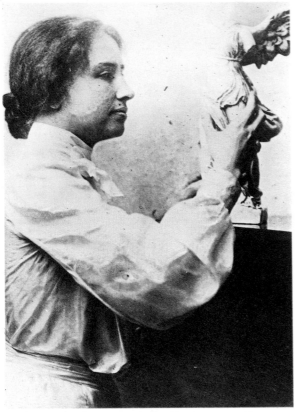

Helen "sees" a statue through her fingers.

At the start of 1914, Helen made a lecture tour of America. To the crowds who came to see her she seemed "the sweetest, finest, noblest spirit in the world." But it was not an easy tour, for Annie's marriage was breaking up. Helen would greatly miss John Macy's support and friendship.

When war broke out in Europe, Helen did not support either side.

But some people thought she favored Germany, since she claimed that Europe's "most bloodthirsty man" was not the German Kaiser, but the Czar of Russia. "Every war has for me the horror of a family feud," she said. She felt that the workers of the nations at war could gain nothing from fighting each other, and that American workers should go on strike against United States involvement.

When America entered the war in 1917, many of her friends who held radical political views, were rounded up and jailed. But Helen remained defiant. She reacted to news of the Russian Revolution, in the same year, with joy, and claimed proudly: "I am a Socialist and a Bolshevik."

In 1918, Helen's life was made into a film, called *Deliverance*. It was a thrilling experience to be in Hollywood, and to meet film stars like Charlie Chaplin, Mary Pickford, Lillian Gish and Douglas Fairbanks. In the film's later scenes, Helen acted herself. *Deliverance* contained some very fanciful scenes, showing her as a

"Joan of Arc" character, leading humanity to a better world.

But unfortunately, the film was not a commercial success. Soon, "to make money," as she frankly admitted, Helen began to appear with Annie in vaudeville theater shows. Audiences were fascinated to see them act out "the miracle" – Helen's first sudden understanding of W-A-T-E-R.

And they were delighted by her quick wit in answering questions.

Following this, she made many successful fund-raising tours for the American Foundation for the Blind. She also wrote two more books – one about her religion (Swedenborgianism) called *My Religion*, and one called *Midstream*, which brought her life story up to date.

(From left to right) *Helen, Annie and Polly Thomson.*

Gentle companions

During the early 1930s, Annie's health began to decline. Increasingly, Helen became dependent on the day-to-day assistance of Polly Thomson, who had joined their household some twenty years before. Annie's greatness as a teacher was widely recognized, and when Helen was awarded an honorary degree by Temple University in 1931, Annie was persuaded to accept a degree as well.

The three women traveled widely, visiting Britain and Ireland, France and Yugoslavia.

Helen "listened" to music on the radio by feeling the vibrations through the case.

They stayed with Polly's family in Scotland, and were received by the King and Queen at Buckingham Palace. Helen continued to work energetically on behalf of the blind: the Helen Keller Endowment Fund, and a

World Conference for the Blind, did much to advance their cause.

If she had been given just three days to see, Helen wrote, on the third day she would explore "the workaday world" of the city; on the second day it would be museums – to see "the condensed history of the earth and its inhabitants"; but on the first day she would want to see "the people whose kindness, gentleness and companionship have made my life worth living."

Annie Sullivan, Helen's closest companion, had become almost blind herself during her final years. In October 1936, she died. For Helen, "it was as if the fire of Teacher's mind, through which I had so vividly experienced the light, the music, and the glory of life had been withdrawn." But Helen was determined to continue her public career, no matter how hard this might prove to be without Annie at her side.

In 1937, with Polly, Helen made a spectacularly successful tour of Japan. Thousands turned out to see her, and she was invited to meet the Emperor and Empress, too. Polly wrote that Helen was making history – that her speeches were advancing the cause not only of the handicapped,

For almost fifty years, Annie had been at Helen's side, teaching and guiding her.

but also of women in Japan. But before they left, Japan began launching attacks on China. Once again, the world was building up to war.

"A light in the darkness"

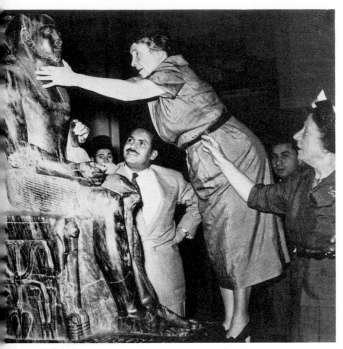

Feeling an ancient statue in Egypt.

As early as 1931, Helen had believed in the likelihood of another war. She had met Albert Einstein, the great scientist, and joined his group of people who intended to resist fighting another war. But as she came to understand what Fascism meant, she decided that war was justified. She declared that it was better to fight than submit to systems of government that "murder the soul and destroy human rights."

During World War II, Helen spent much of her time visiting wounded soldiers in American military hospitals. She wrote that these tours were "the crowning experience" of her life. She brought great comfort and hope, especially to those who had been blinded. At this time, too, she made a special appeal on behalf of black blind people – who, she said, were one of the "least cared-for" groups of all.

After 1945, she made many more foreign tours, raising money for the blind. Visiting Japan once again, she went to Hiroshima and Nagasaki, cities which had been destroyed by nuclear weapons. "It has scorched a deep scar in my soul," she said – and she pledged "to fight against the demons of

Helen and Polly on a visit to London.

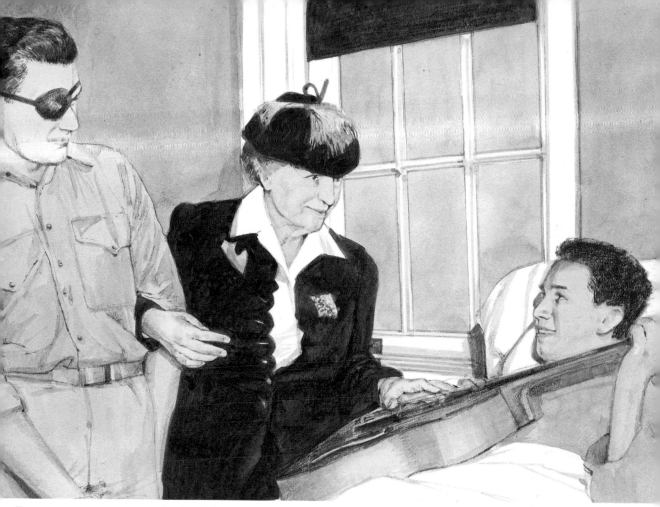

Encouraging a wounded soldier during World War II.

atomic warfare."

Helen's tours covered the globe, from Australasia, the Far East and South America, to South Africa, the Middle East and India. Her life was the subject of films and books, and her name was familiar to millions all around the world. At the age of seventy-five, she was the first woman ever to receive an honorary degree from Harvard University. And she wrote one more book, *Teacher*, about Annie, who had come, so many years before, "to reveal all things" to her.

In 1961 Helen Keller was forced by ill-health to retire from public life. Slowly, in the devoted care of her family and friends, her final years passed. She died on June 1, 1968. Helen's legacy to the world was, above all, a triumphant life story that will continue to inspire people for generations to come.

Dates and events

1880	Helen's birth in Tuscumbia, Alabama (June 27).
1882	She becomes deaf and blind as a result of an unidentified illness.
1887	Anne Sullivan arrives as Helen's teacher. Helen discovers language – W-A-T-E-R: "the miracle."
1888	Her first visit to the Perkins Institution for the Blind.
1891	*The Frost King*.
1894	She enters a school for the deaf in New York.
1896	Helen discovers the teachings of Emanuel Swedenborg. She enters the Cambridge School for Young Ladies.
1900–04	Studies at Radcliffe College.
1903	*The Story of My Life* published.
1905	Anne Sullivan marries John Macy.
1906	Works with the blind of Massachusetts.
1908	*The World I Live In* published.
1909	She joins the Socialist Party.
1913	*Out of the Dark* published.
1914	Arrival of Polly Thomson.
1915	Helen joins the National Women's Party.
1918–19	*Deliverance* filmed in Hollywood. Vaudeville appearances.
1924	Helen begins work for the American Foundation for the Blind.
1927	*My Religion* published.
1929	*Midstream: My Later Life* published.
1930–33	Visits to Britain, Ireland, France and Yugoslavia.
1931	Honorary degree from Temple University.
1936	Anne Sullivan Macy dies.
1937	Tour of Japan.
1942	United States enters World War II. Helen visits wounded soldiers.
1946	Visits European countries fund-raising for the American Foundation for the Overseas Blind.
1948–52	Further tours, to Australia, New Zealand, Japan, South Africa and the Middle East.
1953	*The Unconquered*, a documentary film about Helen. Visit to Latin America.
1955	*Teacher* published. Visits to India and Japan. Honorary degree from Harvard University.
1957	Visit to Scandinavia. *The Miracle Worker*, a play and later a film about Helen and Annie, is first performed.
1960	Polly Thomson dies.
1961	Helen's health declines. She retires from public life.
1968	Helen Keller dies (June 1).

Glossary

Birth control Methods used to restrict child bearing.

Bolshevik A revolutionary – someone who supported the Russian leaders Lenin and Trotsky.

Braille A system of writing for the blind, consisting of raised dots that can be interpreted by touch. Invented by Louis Braille (1802–52).

Capital punishment Punishment by death for a crime.

Child labor The full-time employment of children.

Fascism A political movement founded by the Italian leader Mussolini, in the 1920s. It inspired other movements which encourage militarism and opposition to democracy (freely elected governments).

Inauguration The ceremony of swearing-in the President of the United States.

Joan of Arc A saint, and national heroine of France, who led an army against the invading English.

Militant To be aggressive or vigorous in support of a cause.

Radcliffe College A women's college linked with Harvard University, in Cambridge, Massachusetts.

Radical Favoring extreme change in systems of government, social conditions, etc.

Red flag A symbol of Socialism, Communism or revolution.

Socialism The belief that a country's wealth (resources) should belong to all the people and not to individual private owners, and that the state should control and decide how these resources should be used.

Socialist Party A political party which supports socialism.

Southern belle A young woman of beauty and refinement, from a southern state of the U.S.

Swedenborgianism A religion based on the teachings of Emanuel Swedenborg (1688–1772), the founder of the New Church.

Vaudeville Variety shows, especially popular in the early 20th century.

"Wobblies" Nickname given to members of the I.W.W. (International Workers of the World) Union.

Books to Read

Davidson, Margaret. *Helen Keller: Centennial Edition*. New York: Hastings, 1980.

Gibson, William. *The Miracle Worker*. New York: Bantam.

Keller, Helen. *The Story of My Life*. New York: Airmont.

Sabin, Francene. *The Courage of Helen Keller*. Mahwah, NJ: Troll Associates, 1982.

Index

Picture credits